PEABODIO'S JOKE TRON

640 JOKES

by Peabodio

ISBN: 0-7596-1777-5

This book is printed on acid free paper.

1stBooks - rev. 04/10/02

Special thanks to the entire cast of SNL 1995-2000. Except for two of you.

Thanks to D.W., Al, Trey, Peabody Clouser, Ed, Anthony Gucci, Jedd, Todd, Phil, Pete, Dave, Doug Raye, Dirty-D, Double-D, Gary Dontzig, Gary Douglas Peabody, Gary Doug Key, Gus, Jesus, Dick, Rich, Deb M., Kitty, Kutty K., Hobo Reporter & the HC cast, Douglas Garry & his brother, PGD, daughter, Clouser, everyone at Laughtrack of America and GDPC.

Thanks to Universal for allowing me to grow up finally after making up all those names on American Pie and End Of Days.

TABLE OF CONTENTS

CHAPTER ONE

POLITICAL

Here comes justice, like a Grey snake from the clouds, issuing punishment and distruction wherever it goes. Learning the righteous distraught from the sinister posterity.

Have you heard the judges and prosecutors sending someone to jail just for a kick? Why does every governor laugh at that? They all do.

Then she said, "He creeps them up just for a joke." It's true Mrs. Bush.

When I turn on the radio and I hear them talking about Bush and Gore, I am not sure if they are talking about political candidates or the latest Hollywood movie feature.

All Bush wants to know is since Gore is using the presidential campaign to launch his music career, which career should we take seriously?

Peabodio

Dullness is not only the energy of politics, it is the energy of television. I promise never to be dull.

I am going to the Catholic bar and tell them you made a pass at the rough end.

The newsroom did roar with laughter through when I asked, “Well I can’t stand it. Who’s winning the German or the Jew?”

I am not a commie you know. I am very different. I like to tease the wealthy and find out why they are not all queers.

Relax and feel good royal realms. I am a collie and I prance like a horse.

Losing God is so every bit of a blow. It’s something they will all have to live with.

Did ya know that the federal government will not continuously hire relatives. At some point this will stop. After two generations and five family members you'll be told, "No more for yours." Or "Two per family limit per generation. Three generation maximum."

Yeah south. Has this happened to you? Going along with the round you provoke the yankee by saying something ridiculous. The confeder thuggery comes around and pats you on the back. Exstorts twenty dollars from you.

Because the men put their minds together though, they'd be sent to hell too. That leaves some old churchlady who claims to be a descendant of Jesus lingering on the minds of females. She'll bother then all to wash something in the sink, raise the blinds everyday and wipe the dust up.

I refused the preacher at one time. He gave up on telling me that I was going to hell. He now calls me a yak.

I didn't want to give money to the poor. The churchman called me names, like the Hispanics do. Then they put their minds together and came up with another name for people who really aren't Jewish and they'd call them Protestants. Which was their way of consealing that they really meant whores.

You know how those near the bishop give out blessings? When they get to hear the cronically ill they say, “Quicker dreams.”

It is not true that mission bells have something to do with hooped skirts. It is also not true that Protestants, brought in as laborors, made bells.

Have you seen the planned capitol city of Brazila? All the Brazilians need is a national policy to go with it.

That’s what your afraid of. That your bribing people. Yeah well it worked in France. Scrapping the gold.

If you know where my brother now lives then you know why Pamela calls and urges them to say things they might regret into a microphone.

In case your not sure, I treat religion as if it was political. That’s because the U.S.A. accepts the Vatacan as a country.

Does this mean that the dope doesn't cuss?

If the Chinese say that they're Indonesian and leave us out of it. They must have failed to win their support that time.

Some of you are angry about how the medieval surfdom became slavery all over the world at about the same time as well, in our so great history. It all can be blamed on Henry the Eighth. Anyone who executes his wives like that. Oh come on. Then there are the songs of Henley.

Have a new me. If your white you won't get it. They laugh if you bring it up.

They're not our titles Henry the Eighth. They're all yours. So is my daughter if she pleases him and that saves my head. Nore is that not the way people are today with movie moguls.

Peabodio

A female friend stared at me, covered one eye with one hand and shook her head. So I said, “Nice of her to acknowledge that I am a moderate.”

Make money off politicians, why not?

I’ve often thought the only use the neighborhood mothers had for this man was to obtain jobs for hucks.

If the election comes down to a tie, does the U.S. allow for flipping the coin?

I am a Christian. Because of my name, are you trying to figure out which one I am Catholic or Protestant? Oh, which one should I be today?

So who gets the Irish to sing the old jigs? It is always the English yes.

Why wasn't I arrested in Russia during the second revolution you ask? The soldiers took bribes.

Well is he not like Jesus? The way that hobo walks around helping people when they won't help themselves.

These lambs to the slaughter. Here lion lion lion. Fresh Christians!

Black people joke: I can't be me, they say. I am black people.

His family traditional comment was, "Happy horse shit." What was yours?

He goes to dale and says he's there. They never bug his pretrial cell like they'd bug ours. So they never find out.

We accept that some of you are paranoid that the southerns are going to invade your neighborhood.

Why are black people the only people that make sense to me today? As if to say the thinking of the others is off.

So who gets the head of the committee jobs when the congress is fifty percent Republican and fifty percent Democrat? I guess flipping the coin is out of the question.

So to those Nationalists who are still left in the world and to those that see little animals in the ink blots, your fine.

Have you ever watched daytime talk shows? Sounds more like a an argument. One of the volunteers to be the good soul kicked into it o.k.? He discovered that his record was good experience.

Even though I thanked Jesus in my book, I admit I got ripped off by the Devil.

Can you believe the way the Democrats can get away with money laundering laughing in the face of the Republicans? If one dollar was missing from a Republican campaign, the press used to go on and on about it.

Reenpants knows no more about the economy than you or I. In fact even before the first term of his appointment he ask certain people for their opinion on what he should do about the interest rate. Hobo was one of them. How smart could that be? Really, this man has no brain. Truth is I couldn't stand the way this man is still in office. Please appoint a new person.

Let's see. Killing civilians, that's really bad senator. Was it a much different feeling when you downed the helicopter your wive's former husband was riding in? This all makes sense in light of the fact that the chorus lyrics for that show were taken from me.

I wouldn't give Jesus air time because he wouldn't pay me. Just like XBC.

You wants eye to eye themselves until they don't hear or come out!

You say to VP Cheney, "You know about the diseases he has."

The kingdoms don't exist anymore. The foreigners thrown out. The government can give them back their titles whenever it wants to.

Peabodio

May drunk discount ski packages come your way. They get it.

Teenagers are enough of a problem without them clogging our drainage system.

So I retired to my home Dunbarton Oaks and contemplated my next career move.

While chasing Russians that fell from the sky, you've done nothing to further your way on earth. Some of us thought it was possible to leave something in orbit up there.

You haven't experienced Mexico until the police ask, "What is your business here?"

You've heard about that guy over there Wills? Well when he found out he fell from Charles II, he must have decided to out do him. Number of felled females? Ten!

Lizzie Borden killed her victim with an ax in Fall River MA, yet the court would not convict her. It set a precedent and women are still getting away with murder in New England to this day.

CHAPTER TWO

OPPOSITE SEX

Everywhere I went I was followed by my clevage. I say I am not my clevage.

Girls seldom make passes at guys that wear glasses.

Remember the headlines, “Magaga And Baby Cheat!” Whatever. This is new ground for her.

It’s typical of women to spend half their time trying to find out about women too. Why?

We know you gals only need a few muscles guys around and all the vaginas are taken care of.

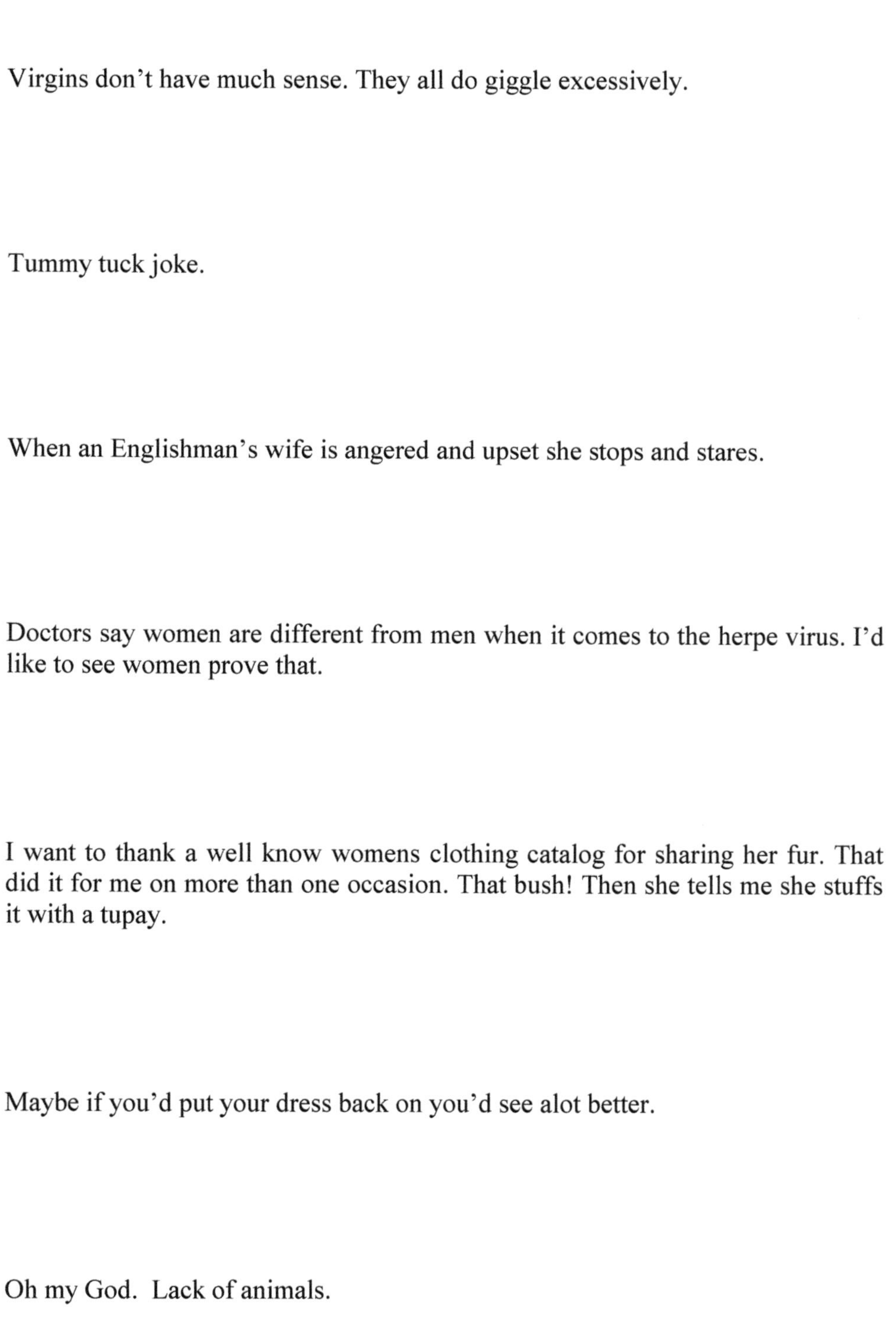

Virgins don't have much sense. They all do giggle excessively.

Tummy tuck joke.

When an Englishman's wife is angered and upset she stops and stares.

Doctors say women are different from men when it comes to the herpe virus. I'd like to see women prove that.

I want to thank a well know womens clothing catalog for sharing her fur. That did it for me on more than one occasion. That bush! Then she tells me she stuffs it with a tupay.

Maybe if you'd put your dress back on you'd see alot better.

Oh my God. Lack of animals.

Peabodio

I stand before you here today knees trembling in graditute.

Hey Roll-n-roll Magazine and consider the son photo she was. You've really done it to me this time. My circiuts are definitely up.

Then your mother gives one of those gifts that you have to use however tells you someday you will. Your tendency is to take it back, trade it in or give it away.

The rest of us are left afraid that at least little things she'll yell rakes for all. So she really has to take us by the hand.

Your an unlikely husband and apparently you've got a successful marriage. What's your secret? Honesty, integrity and dammed excellent lies.

It's true. I've called her names that rhyme with Hornchow. The others were designed to make her feel special.

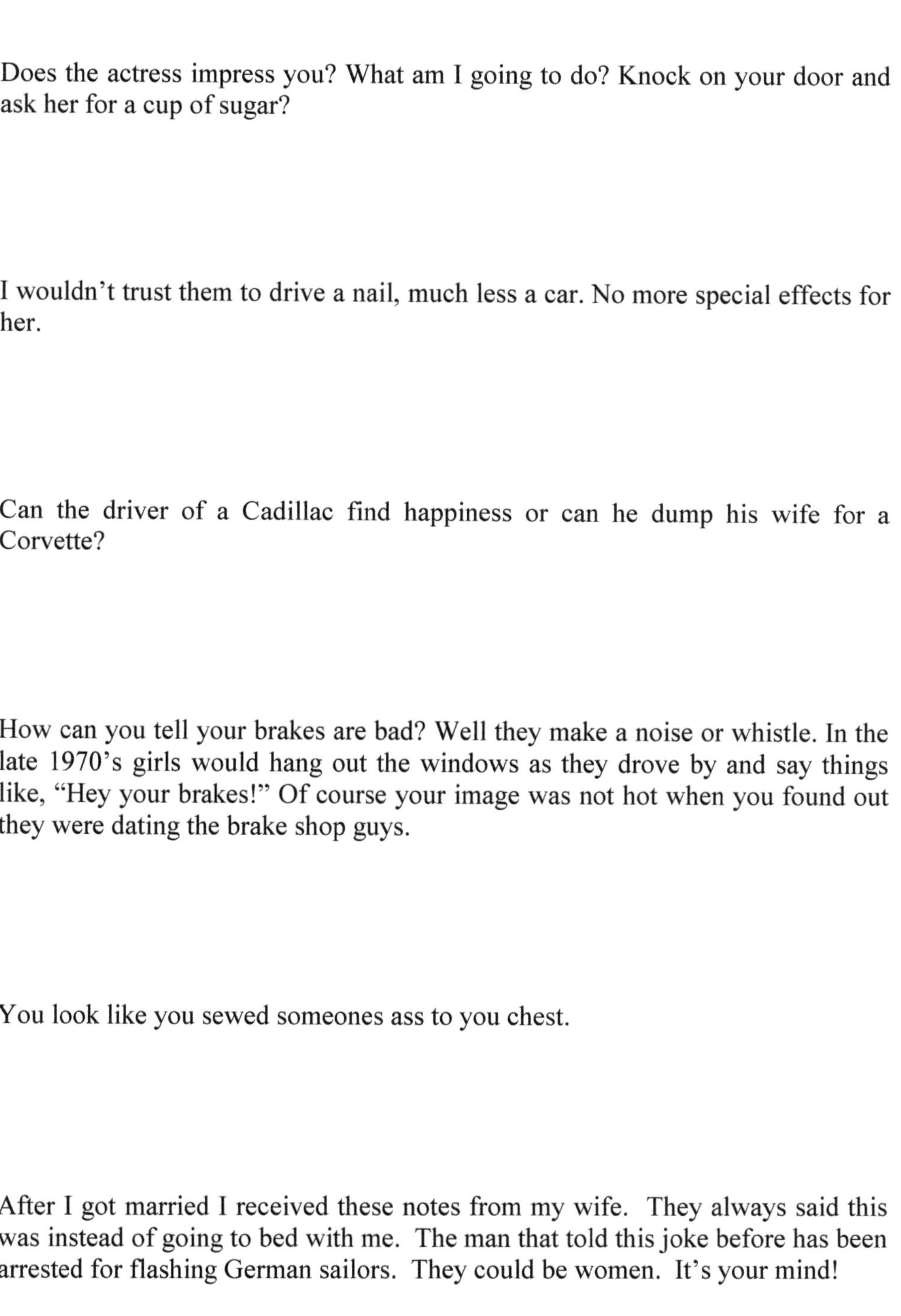

Does the actress impress you? What am I going to do? Knock on your door and ask her for a cup of sugar?

I wouldn't trust them to drive a nail, much less a car. No more special effects for her.

Can the driver of a Cadillac find happiness or can he dump his wife for a Corvette?

How can you tell your brakes are bad? Well they make a noise or whistle. In the late 1970's girls would hang out the windows as they drove by and say things like, "Hey your brakes!" Of course your image was not hot when you found out they were dating the brake shop guys.

You look like you sewed someones ass to you chest.

After I got married I received these notes from my wife. They always said this was instead of going to bed with me. The man that told this joke before has been arrested for flashing German sailors. They could be women. It's your mind!

You know it's so typical of the media to switch the labels and have fun in the wake of females chasing the money trail.

She got fired from the Tom McCann's for using the foot measurer inappropriately.

Get your poodle wet and nasty. Tie tie to tie tie hungry.

My sister caused Avon stock to rise in the 1970's

She thinks she's perverted me simply by touching my butt.

Shirt. I am the guy who got cherry to chirp

Suzanne Harbee? Snif snif.

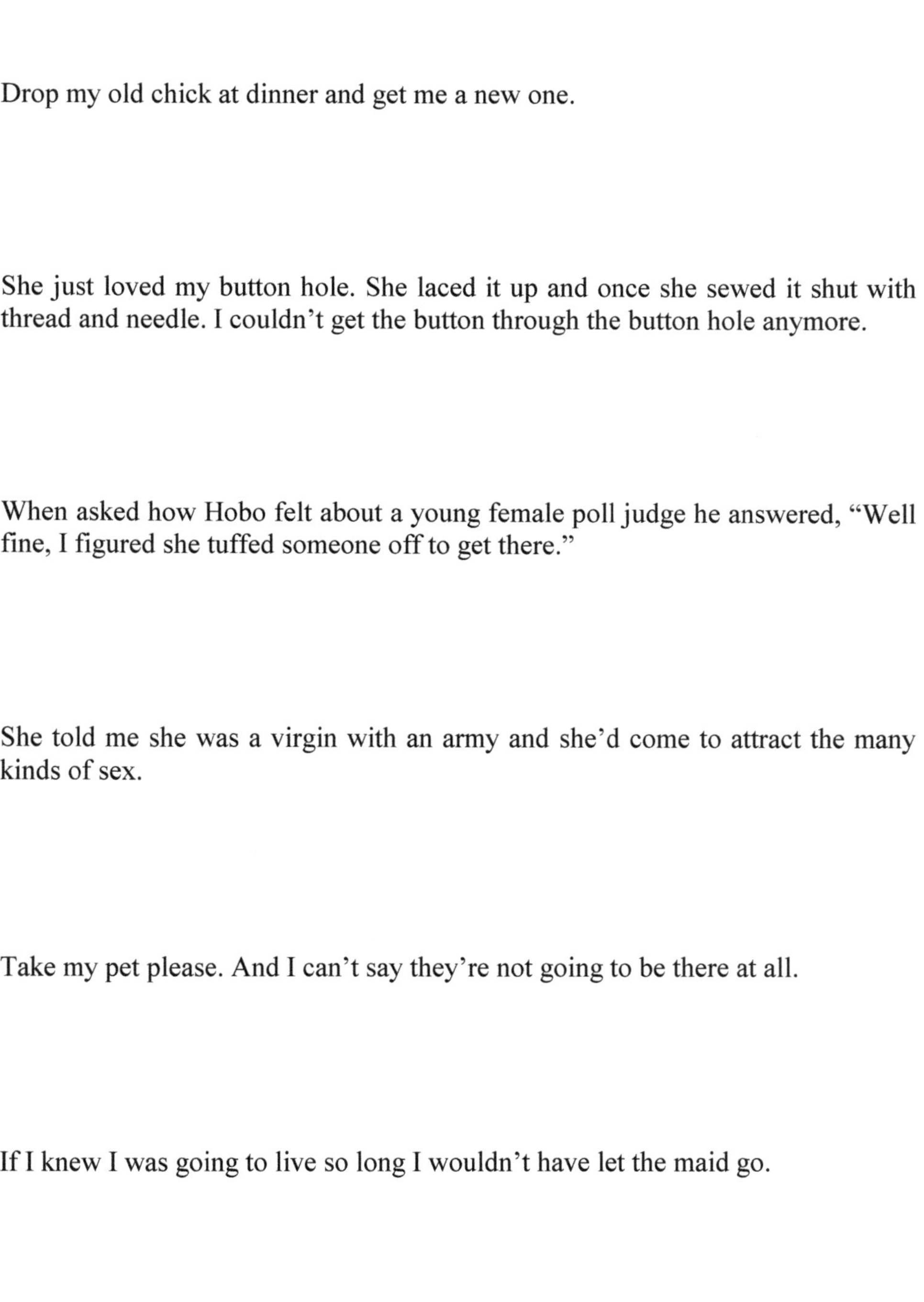

Drop my old chick at dinner and get me a new one.

She just loved my button hole. She laced it up and once she sewed it shut with thread and needle. I couldn't get the button through the button hole anymore.

When asked how Hobo felt about a young female poll judge he answered, "Well fine, I figured she tuffed someone off to get there."

She told me she was a virgin with an army and she'd come to attract the many kinds of sex.

Take my pet please. And I can't say they're not going to be there at all.

If I knew I was going to live so long I wouldn't have let the maid go.

Peabodio

Once again, it's not the way it wants to say it does.

Granddad use to say to pregnant women that giving birth to children was almost as easy for them as it was for a cow or a horse.

Rita says men stink and they should all die. She's not confused. That ain't the way to have fun.

I win. I am the golden goddess of television. Oh wow, truth hurts. Cry baby.

I have to go scrub my ass because your coming over latter to kiss it.

You don't know your ass from a toboggan.

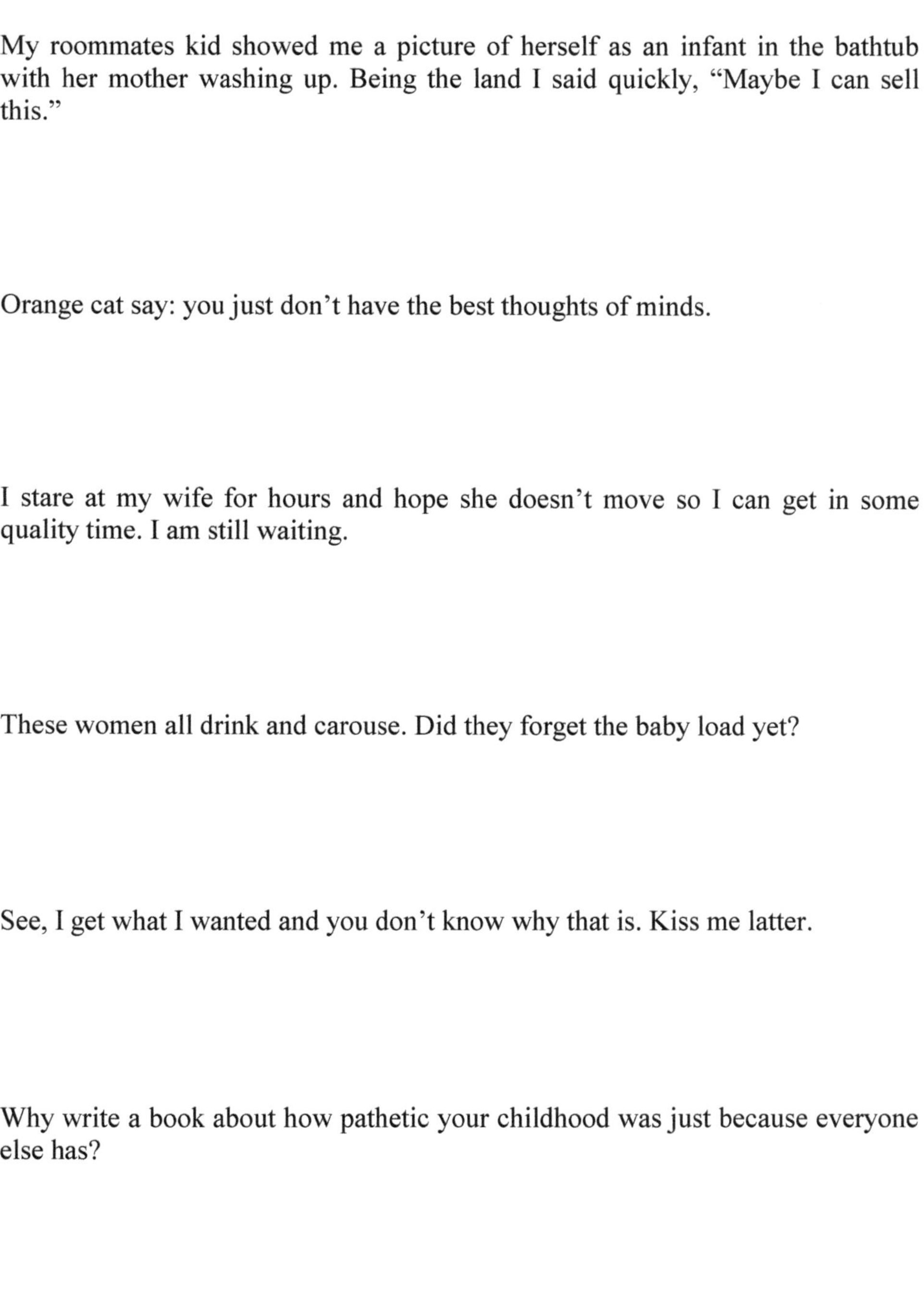

My roommates kid showed me a picture of herself as an infant in the bathtub with her mother washing up. Being the land I said quickly, "Maybe I can sell this."

Orange cat say: you just don't have the best thoughts of minds.

I stare at my wife for hours and hope she doesn't move so I can get in some quality time. I am still waiting.

These women all drink and carouse. Did they forget the baby load yet?

See, I get what I wanted and you don't know why that is. Kiss me latter.

Why write a book about how pathetic your childhood was just because everyone else has?

Peabodio

Any room of women is worst then a pack of drifters. Your being conned by the worst of.

On next. Attack of the desert.
The father's English. The Irish were up more then one of the wives. One wonders if it was the same Irish with every wife?

What are you doing? Packing stuff. It's what you turned into after your ballet career fell through.

Why do some pilots call them waitresses?

I don't know. I never know. I will not let you think I know.

You know what those female architects are like? Was she going to marry him and then kiss him for half the firm or just hate him for his friends luggage from the start?

Know her? Does anybody really know anybody?
Hobo said that every time they swerve closer. Soon we'll have a confirmed death.

Park Avenue trailhead.

About the Million Mom March on Mother's Day 5.00 Hobo said, "I don't blame them. They seen to be using diesel trucks and poison food to take their husbands out anyway."

Women don't know what it means, what his life.

A little upset today. She found out her real weight.

All men want to know why we can't treat women the same way we treat men. Given equal time and all, except for the sex and all.
Give me sex now or I'll kick your ass doesn't mean your an abuse victim if you don't find that funny.

Between whitening stick and cosmetic surgery. I feel like [Use anyone's name here.]

When you put on the leopard, it growls. Orange Kat.

He's a male cat and he knows what women like. He's waiting for you at home that's all.

Kick it homie all the way!

I'll also bet you ladies say that to your husbands when you get divorced.

I'll bet the only reason you wanted a pet was to watch it lick weenie!

Retractable head.

Some guys would say she needs a hug. Then she pulls out a gun.

The male real estate agents are nearly as much trouble as the women. Even that agent from ... was on a leash.

The guy is so built and thinks he looks like God. You'd expect a couple of babies should be sucking on his pecs.

You've heard of arranged marriages? Her papa told me if I was interested, she was all mine. He was sure of it up until the lady insulted me. You could be sure she was forever.

Because you got the hoest conversation. Yours ruin the nation.

Hey ladies! It's time to get yourself to POWERED PEAK PARK.

Parents, set your kids straight. Most flirting occurs in the subway. Not during spring break.

Warning! Listening to women could get you killed, bentaled or jailed! Think for yourself! Can you?

He's gonna break your fate if you don't stop biting your nails and spiting them out. Find a pretty girl to do that.

Your daughter says, "Dad, I'am a virgin o.k.?" Does that mean she is one or isn't one?

Have you seen my wife? She has a big fat nasty butt. Several of the fetus people live inside it. They pay her rent money.

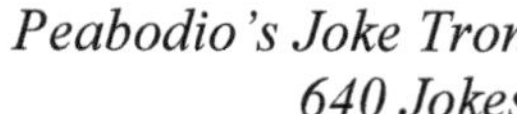

Remember if she black and she dising like this, she's warting off all those white devils floating around you.

Mom tells me Dad was a roadie but she was too drunk and doesn't remember which one.

So women really watch each others purses. Fruit patrol cat women caught a coody.

Cloris was so sick of being ignored by men that she picked on you as a hobby.

Blackie and Blondie promotion space wanted. She got busted for her beauty o.k.?

In Illinois, they have this saying. Looking for on loud hit.

Are there any Ramone roadies out there still living that haven't scaved for a keg? It really really really…

In golf, ninety-five is not a bad score. If I avoid the windmills, I do just fine.

To the French bread who took my underwear out of the dryer when I was at the public laundry. Keep that. It might be worth money someday.

New York chicks spring for tax. Fair, if they don't want it! Shoot, I am use to paying for dinner, movie and breakfast and still not getting anything, and I've been married for seven years.

And in 1857, witches spells no longer made them any uglier. Call 1-800-Joke tron.

My ex-wife designed my office. I had to put some of it in a box and keep it in the storage. Some of you gals know it was too much clutter. The key people would have come in and been there all day inventing ways to keep me away. She had the nerve to ask for that box at the settlement. My prized valuables.

Walking amongst the dune one day, I happened upon a buried ice box. Opening the door was the equivalent to finding treasure to my four-year-old grandchild. I said to the proprietor, "Well we found the ice box that went to the cottage we rented and you said the mobile was brought in to replace it. We were lucky since they were booked all the way up to Wildbury City. Oh yeah, the ice box was empty. The contents claimed by the sea. The name of the cottage colony was "Sea Drift".

It's the kind of house that makes them paranoid. Not only that but they can look up her dress.

Her only claim to fame is erecting men. Like Jack Daniels.

On this day Carolynn's car flipped over and blew up, killing her, her lesbian lover and the kidnapped son of a Protestant clergyman.

My mom has just told me she can't believe you wore white on your wedding day. Then you wouldn't mind if we refer to your raised glass as the wicked clink.

Well, your just a regular Miss Congeniality.

Peabodio

When they open the doors to the sale you know how it is ladies. You have no friends.

I don't really gamble too much. They've got some woman following me.

Maybe you used to work at Shania's Coastal Cone and Doughnut.

For some women confidence is a flighty thing. It's like P.M.S.! It comes, it goes.

Step dancing. That is ice in Swiss clothes doing Swiss clogging and pretending it is their heritage.

Once again, it's not the way it wants to say it does.

CHAPTER THREE

LINERS

O.k. little six year old Shania, I'll protect you from the splinter people.

I am the King of Lenister. Prepare to invade. Set up the defenses and stare at them all. In that way I will crush them down.

Don't insult folks. Lean back, take a deep breath and think of a better way to keep them all confused. Shut up. Don't debate.

I wouldn't mind a country place that's falling to me from a bogus relation. You know, the one with the long driveway, crop in the field. There wouldn't be much to do there. We could grow Shannon's thought. Do you know someone with the name?

For those of you who need to know. Actors are all so nice on the way up. This is before they remember that there's something about you.

Peabodio

I grew up in Utah. The state is run by the Morman church. Yeah, Salt Lake squirrel town.

She looks over to him and says, "It should be longer then that."

In the northeast they warn you not to get close because of the bad gas. In Utah, they'd only warn you not to get close because of the bad gas too. They'd say something like, "Oh well."

Have you ever looked out and seen the boot? In the trees or in the clouds? It calls me.

These are jokes. Not a tractor-trailer mishap.

Theft is the way to power. That's why the police have to be in charge of it. That was said by some cop up there.

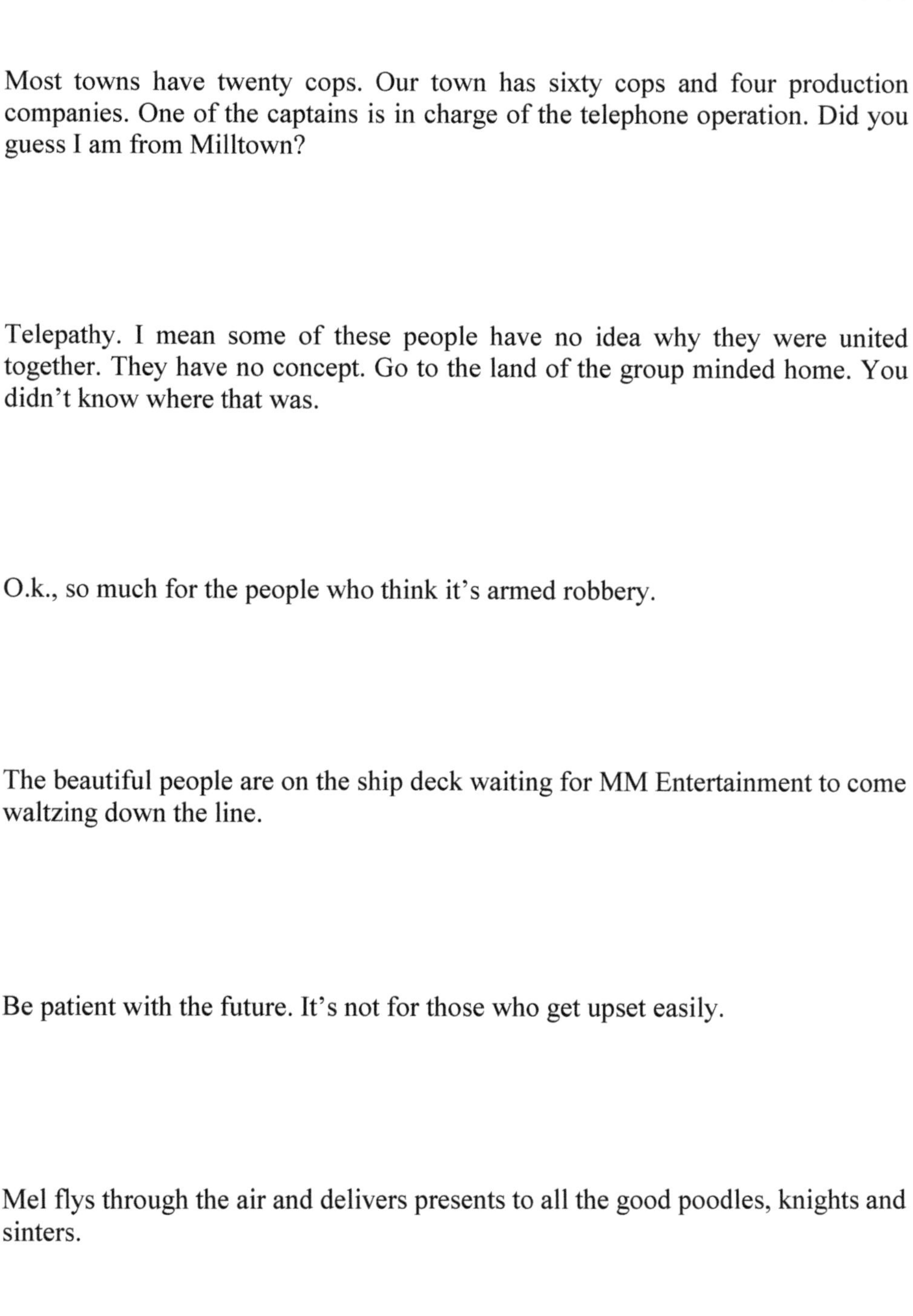

Most towns have twenty cops. Our town has sixty cops and four production companies. One of the captains is in charge of the telephone operation. Did you guess I am from Milltown?

Telepathy. I mean some of these people have no idea why they were united together. They have no concept. Go to the land of the group minded home. You didn't know where that was.

O.k., so much for the people who think it's armed robbery.

The beautiful people are on the ship deck waiting for MM Entertainment to come waltzing down the line.

Be patient with the future. It's not for those who get upset easily.

Mel flys through the air and delivers presents to all the good poodles, knights and sinters.

Don't sound like that comedy because if you do, he'll find you and start throwing you around again.

One hundred-thousand villages.

Sax warns me about adding piano.

Putting the wind up their robes from inside.

Some think it's time to privatize the post office. Maybe one of those rich Hollywood producers will bid.

My life's not over yet. Start barfing off that.

Staggered truss bar joist roof. Glass block wall management.

It's no lie.

More than one executive is spinning around in the chair thinking Dorothy, Dorothy, Dorothy, where am I now? Spin second verse.

In case your not sure how the La Braya Tar Pits were formed Ed, it all started when some kid supported a television plug for it instead of the Sidewalk Hall of Fame.

Star stomp wasn't my idea.

It is not true that Ed, who is created with the creation of Star Search, actually came up with the idea for the show. It is true that the man who did was a teenager at the time, and is still outside looking for stars through his telescope.

Peabodio

Mean things your mom says: Clean your room.
Your so dirty and smelly.
Don't stay up late.
No desert for you.

Things your neighbor would do if they caught you making prank telephone calls: They would crush the life out of a fly. They would not hurt anybody's feelings though.

I have an english last name however I am less than one-half English. Condensing the parts, call it one-third.

You know even the French complain about who they can marry. The Italians get off their motorcycles to hunt. Your not an Italian lady o.k.? So am I waiting for Miss Italy? You know natural.

I tolerate fools not at all. Too deep they ain't. If there were two sides of a coin, I'd toss it in the river. I hold nothing but the most and utter contempt.

Yeah. Socks looks Roxanne cheap.

You New York City realtors seem to think that it's worth more money if it faces something green. Where I've totally got that it was worth fifteen dollars a week to be closer to the laundry mat.

Plan on remaining in the New France?

Cheater in marble.

You can do no wrong having come from Chicago.

Dr. Laura also hugs me everytime she sees me.

Well I know you want me to adhere and I don't.

Peabodio

The magician has died.

We hear the Backstreet Boys will invest in a hotel in Huntsville Alabama. Hobo Reporter asks why not set up the top two floors and live there? Since his driving habits suit Alabama and not our state.

I could be half dead or half way to hell.

No fish were named in the making of this book.

[Use Baltimore accent.] I don’t know the family.

So you really didn’t think that was funny?

Something fast makes me dance like crazy.

Metal street factor promises punishment blow. There where iron tooth goes in.

Oh thanks her hale. Once I start talking like this and within a few minutes, I am talking Yonkers.

They call Faye a tolerable and pessky women who stole interior designs.

It's not any of them. Nore always the best of. This one would have done it for me on any one of an ungiven day.

We've clocked it several times. Calling from across the seas. It's thirty-five miles around the house.

Just wait patiently. Nore is his head all full of ideas.

Peabodio

After you've done that you can go straight to L.A.

See you round like a doughnut.

I am too tired like a bicycle.

Only in Denver will you find headlines that read: "Square Dancing Tractors Draw Large Crowds!"

You can save money with many cars not just a volts.

In keeping with Nason. I am descended from Paul.

Punish yourself three times and wait for all the monkeys to fly away.

If you meet one person from New Jersey in your lifetime, your doing really good. If you meet four people from New Jersey chances are you'll get your name in their newspaper.

I can't say I learned nothing at all at that school on New Beer. The thing I learned is the farce. That will teach you backsters to hang on there. Elements of the farce include stairways that go nowhere and a child's doorway so low that insures no adults go there. Of course you'd have to cut the original larger to get it through the code.

There are farms of all kinds for that.

Pennsylvania is a friendly place. Don't ask or follow the directions they give you there or you'll never leave the state.

I hate to be rude and I usually am.

It's the life. You fall down hit the rock hard bottom and then it turns out to be the ledge. Then you fall a bit further.

Even though the Pennsylvanians understand english. They do not speak it.

A talking dog walks into where you are eating dinner. It says, “I wish you knew what you smelled like.”

Impress others with the way you smoke ladies. Exhale through your nose and then breath it back into your mouth. Very classy.

With the news of mercury posioning. I bought a helmet, one air tank and reflective clothing to prevent that planets douse.

Worst then that some female d.j. set out to denouce me as a peer for more then a year. After that I set out to prove it.

When asked, "How are you today?" I had to say, "Well I am having trouble with the one who flys." You might as well sumise I meant a Hollywood actor and a player. That sort of covers it. I tired to say bad things.

I was with you when the amp blew right up until you threw your last pick out as if to feed the crowd.

Next spot you put on the fruitophia. The name of which I invented one day in a radio show waiting room. I got so mad at the reds for not paying me. I made them pull the ad off the air. Then the company pulled the product.

And next it will be taking the hits for seniors.

Oh she was so cute before that truck hit her.

Like you, I also don't think some of these jokes are funny. These are all jokes that you might have heard before. They have got a laugh before.

Oh that was the stariest proposal. Oh my ear.

You don't think this is where we are going but because of Judge Judy- who's tough, we also need Judge Marie- who let's everyone go regardless of what they did do. Frankly all she does is nag.

Some men's groups came forward and asked her to lighten up because judges were adhering her as if she sets precedents.

You'll catch cold if you go nude is a Dutch joke.

I have been sprayed so many times. I am immumed to mase.

Snakeless. You didn't adhere it's a colder and crueler world.

Enjoy it while it lasts but count the lifeboats.

Snake!

Self esteem was always low. He got married just for rice.

That's what Napoleon liked. Little things hitting each other.

The shorter to bore the greatest.

He said he must have fruit.

Fabio was a place for the not too wealthy.

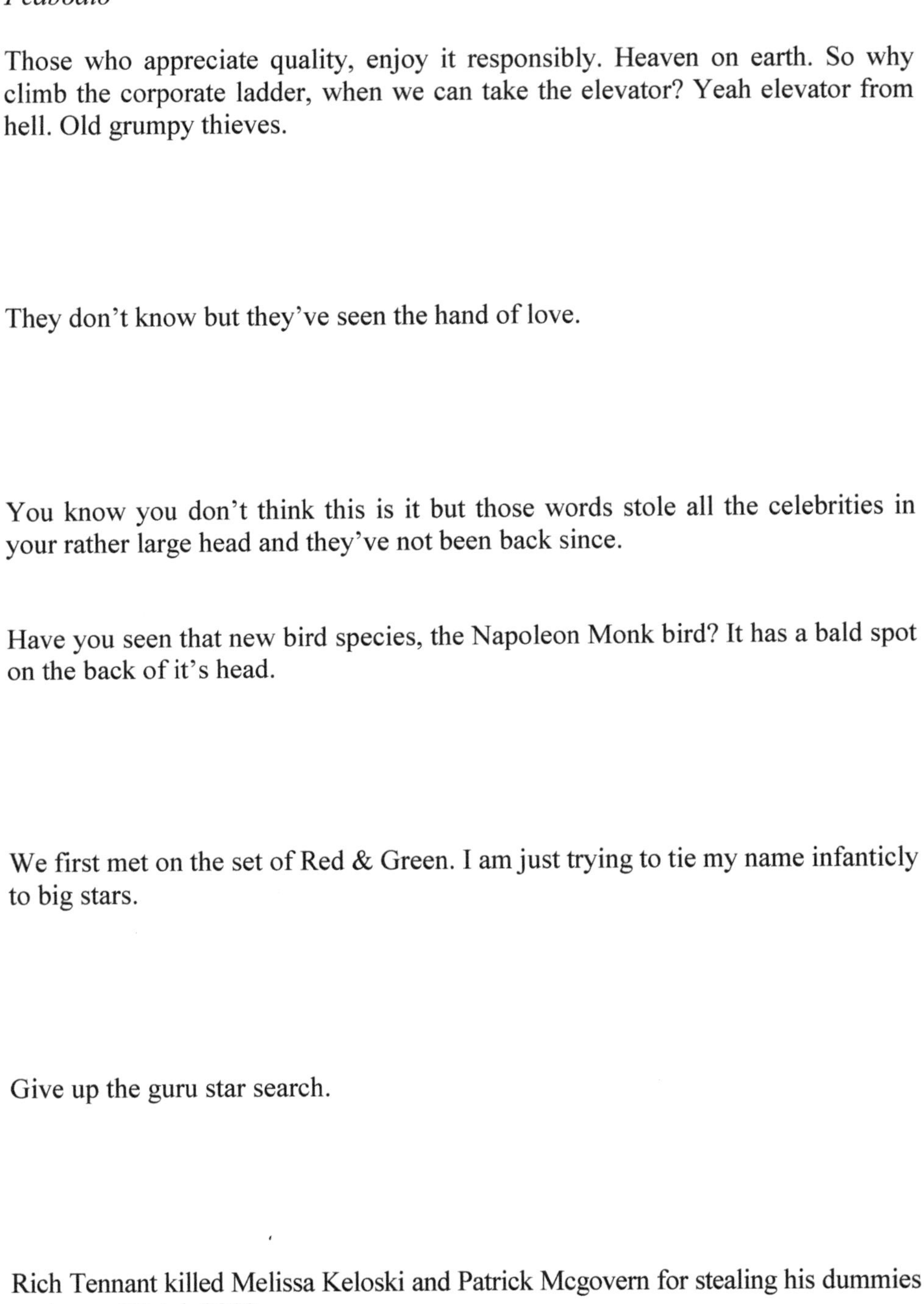

Peabodio

Those who appreciate quality, enjoy it responsibly. Heaven on earth. So why climb the corporate ladder, when we can take the elevator? Yeah elevator from hell. Old grumpy thieves.

They don't know but they've seen the hand of love.

You know you don't think this is it but those words stole all the celebrities in your rather large head and they've not been back since.

Have you seen that new bird species, the Napoleon Monk bird? It has a bald spot on the back of it's head.

We first met on the set of Red & Green. I am just trying to tie my name infanticly to big stars.

Give up the guru star search.

Rich Tennant killed Melissa Keloski and Patrick Mcgovern for stealing his dummies cartoons: Watch 2000.

Old men should stick to hitting on old women.

I get enough bull at work. I don't need to smoke it.

To say anyone arranges time travel is like saying Houdini could untie his shoes.

Son of a...? Better her then somebody I don't know.

Research? We don't even have money in our budget for coffee filters so why are we using paper towels?

That's not exactly not it in a nutshell. That's for real.

Peabodio

Your in danger girl! From bed wetters, thumb suckers and video repairmen.

Parents want to know what to do with a child that hits other children. I've always recommended allowing the larger kids to tackle the boys. Snowballs work on girls, at least in the wintertime.

They have a joke. Once the drugs wear off the music really sucks.

If you go to more then one Dead show without dropping acid, your not paying attention. Things your grandparents have been heard to say.

There are three people following me who want me to drive them around.

A little sincerity is a darn thing. A lot of it and I get downright treacherous.

Your lost in space June. Fly away.

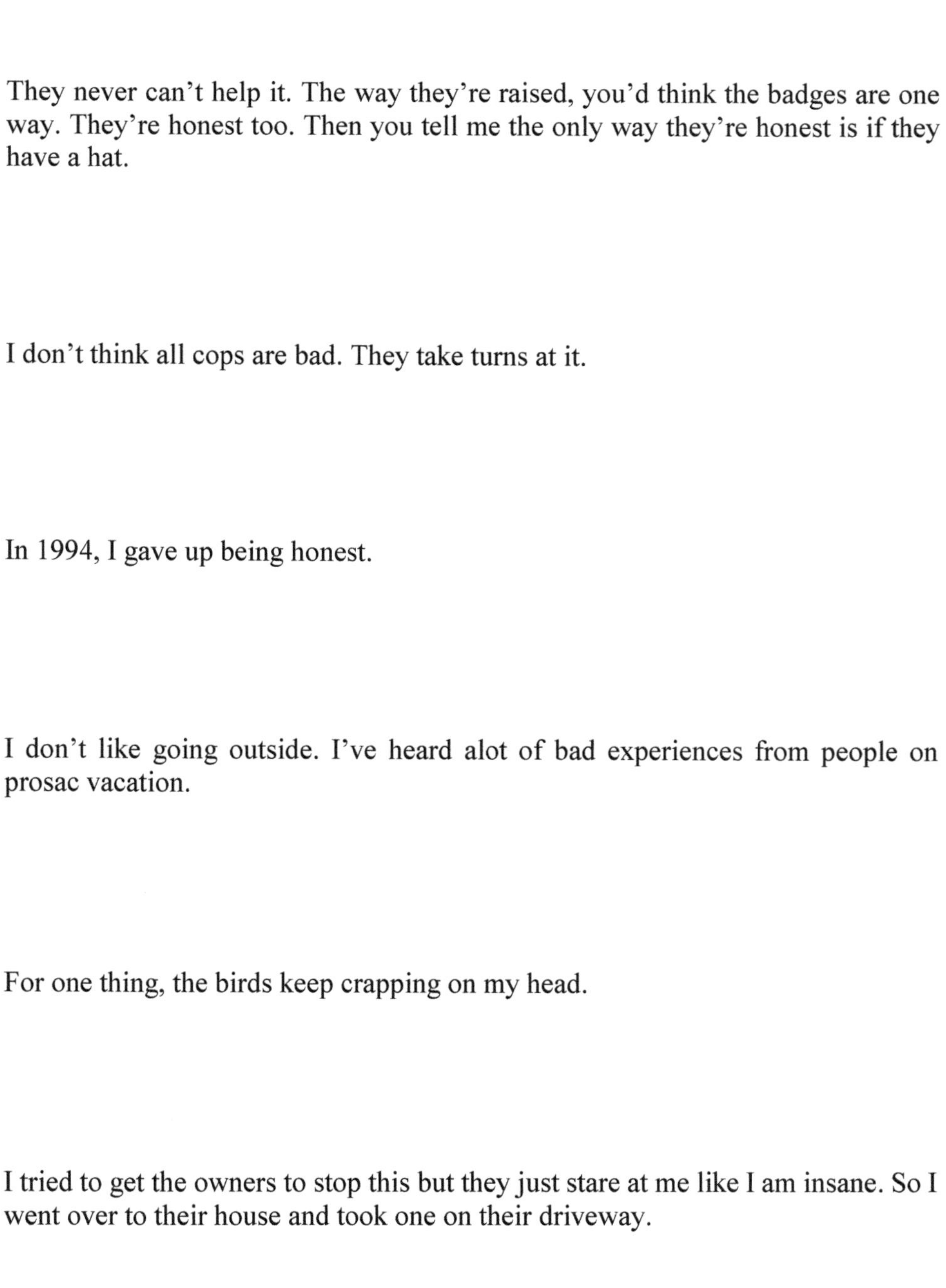

They never can't help it. The way they're raised, you'd think the badges are one way. They're honest too. Then you tell me the only way they're honest is if they have a hat.

I don't think all cops are bad. They take turns at it.

In 1994, I gave up being honest.

I don't like going outside. I've heard alot of bad experiences from people on prosac vacation.

For one thing, the birds keep crapping on my head.

I tried to get the owners to stop this but they just stare at me like I am insane. So I went over to their house and took one on their driveway.

The freshest oceans in the world are in Baha Mexico.

You are the kitty kat. That's right.

Psyco kitty, your so pretty. Guess it shows. I wanna know.

[Say real slow.] My ship was so slow to come in, I took another job as a motivational speaker.

They'll eat their turkey dinner to go at the diner with the others who refused to go anywhere for the holiday.

Does ain't deer. Deer and men. Deer interuptions.

Hey look. It's the four bears. Everyone turns on their televisions at once.

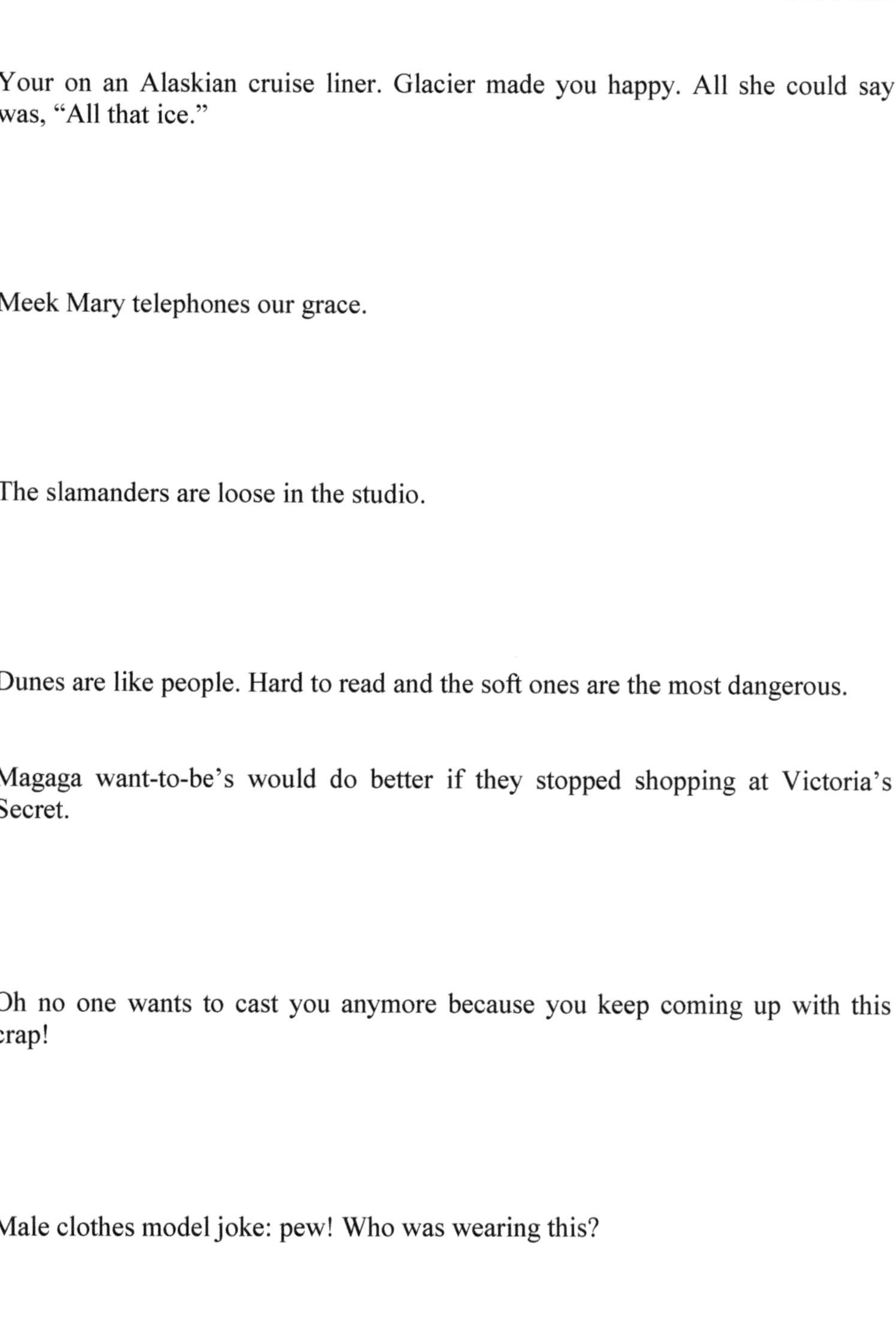

Your on an Alaskian cruise liner. Glacier made you happy. All she could say was, "All that ice."

Meek Mary telephones our grace.

The slamanders are loose in the studio.

Dunes are like people. Hard to read and the soft ones are the most dangerous.

Magaga want-to-be's would do better if they stopped shopping at Victoria's Secret.

Oh no one wants to cast you anymore because you keep coming up with this crap!

Male clothes model joke: pew! Who was wearing this?

Santa Claus can't make it this year so Hobo will be giving out your friends and neighbors gifts.

If you use the telephone I'll break your fingers off! Remember? Do you want your kind to be the way we were? And then dumps it all on dod. In no way ho ho ho!

Musically understood.

Starting next week, women who co-sign loans for criminals.

Flicking picks at the show. It's a lot of fun.

Yeah it's cold. My face is frozen and I can't get my defensive signals out fast enough.

What kind of petting do you like the most? To maul you.

Can't say you know how there's guard over the kitchen samura.

Orange Kat say, you are a lucky lucky man.

I mean his was give me another name please.

Peek a chew is too dicy.

These part jokes.
Well what do you think I've been doing this radio show and not really also a television show for?

Medusa snakes ball of confussion.

She says she boiled tea. I can’t believe she had anyone to do with it except jump in and try to salvage it. That was more then 350 years after they dumped it there.

Take my answering service. Please.

To all aliens: they don’t have rapture in Hollywood.

You have the right to remain.

Bryce Canyon. It’s a hell of a place to lose a cow. Dinosaur reasons.

Angus Jupiter & Engine 119.

Housemates moved. They were a family of three. Left me the cat. I named the cat Cutty Kitty. The names I didn't choose were Reb and Ensign. He's a grey cat so I feed him alot before storms.

There she goes again. My neighbor with her gun to start up the rampage.

Oh come on mister. Your a liar. You recieved only 2,000 tapes for the second show and that's all.

If that's the company guy telling him we need to be more at ease.

Even with your occassional bout of pure evil, it doesn't mean your unloved.

So that happens in the corporate world but I am a hick and that ain't about to happen here.

Bad words! Bad words!

What is wrong with getting married while a teen? The marriage might go bad? Safer than dating.

Assignment: putting in the nationalities can be funny. The other one is, that cities cursed.

Smash it up acme bros.

I dreamed some actors were on the floor looking over the money I dropped. So they saw who I was.

Assignment: make this funny. Cutting a slice of pizza. Measuring the snow with a yard stick. Washing your car with a sponge.

Planet of the Apes could happen.

You know it is so typical of the media to switch the labels and have fun in the wake of the females chasing the money trail.

You know you can count on me to pick the B music for your movie ad Mr. Big shot producer.

We were all raised to answer one of the above. Survey. Sex survey next. After your done filling out our questionnaires pass in the pencils.

It is a picture on transit on one side.

Chicago demon rising up against Charity.

I've got the yard that all the dogs take a crap on.

Huddle kitty.

Peabodio

I get enough bull at work. I don't need to smoke it.

There's no dark side to the moon really. In fact it's all dark.

Rachet stars o.k.? That point got an a plus.

After I revolutionized the music industry, I set out to 1. Cut a demo. 2. Write a joke. 3. Conquer the post office.

Assignment: use grits in a sentence. Kiss my gritty and tell her to kiss mine too.

A little sincerity is superb but alot of to is down right treacherous.

It's the political of drumstick of chicken republic.

A grizzly affair.

The actor was afraid of snakes.

It's no joke, I am so run down all I've got is this leather jacket for a pillow.

Your watching golf. Spending quality time with your cat on your lap. Come on. You guys do that with your dogs too. Somehow, even though you both fell asleep, you manage to get up in time for dinner.

So what do you people with the cups do? After a month of polishing them you have to start over again.
Your kids fight over which trophies they will keep and which ones get melted down after your dead.

Peabodio

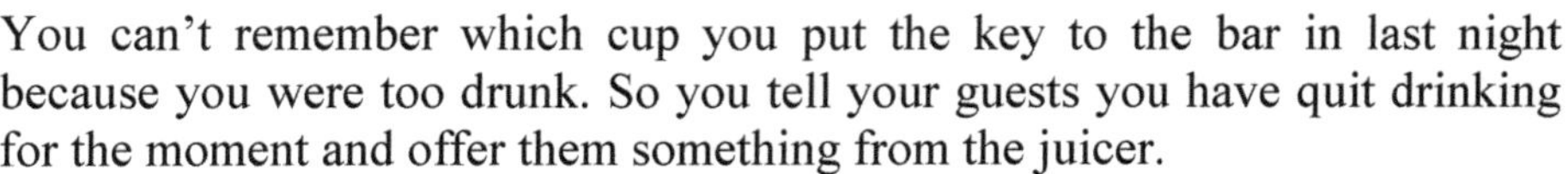

You can't remember which cup you put the key to the bar in last night because you were too drunk. So you tell your guests you have quit drinking for the moment and offer them something from the juicer.

[Sung.] It's my life said the Cutty Kitty.
I don't wanna live in the city.
Compete with rats to stay alive.

Can thrasher dead that tot?

The background vocalist wants to sing to those of you that are on the way up to be millionaires, and those he heard waiting to get on the show.

I am sorry, you want jokes. Want to keep it up. As if I was the willing prunt of jokes. It's plain to see that when it comes to writers, your short and have nothing else.

You are definitely the brother of smugly. When I was in the holding tank you skimmed the burger money and bought me a cheeseburger, pocketing the rest for muscle powder.

Go for the jugular. It's good if you do. Skunks went to a college called Le Pew.

Why aren't there fish in the lake? They just arrived from the government fish farm. Isn't that where all the fish come from?

I'll bet when you open the door kitty's waiting there. He'll run into the room to let you know where he wants to be. So you went in there and sat on the bed and then you heard the cat scream.

Warning! Newspersons who make six digits or more may be pretending to write their own stories!

When I tell them I like their decor, they insult me by making the comment that I somehow have a females taste. So I end up buying the dark colors. Then, they visit and say that I have goth-like taste. You can't win. Are you in retail by chance?

Peabodio

Until this book, my greatest success was failing a lot of screening sessions.

I use green cleaner. I can't help it. My headset includes janitors.

You know what it's like in soccer too. I use to hit some goals in with my head too. I was a kid. The teamates are always elated that we get anything anywhere like that.

I am not patient and I don't understand why I've been here four days.

Come down south of the border. They'll be glad to give you diarrhea.

Sometimes while watching the tube, I've got to look away I stink.

It's like I've always said, I don't take directives from here.

Show us your claws! Well that's what they do. They yawn and stretch.

Beware of this book by Peabodio. It contains alot of warnings disguised as jokes.

A nectie often looks like a fish hanging by the tail.

Italians don't want you to know any national heritages or ethnic group could be subsituted.

Real Italians think your dead if you use a subsitute.

Beautiful pelican. Smelly cut.

Our dear most sacred mackerel.

Some people are afraid to lie under the holy cod.

It's urgently demanded quality time with kitty on lap. He's been jumping onto your kitchen countertop again. When I used to work, kitty would have been dinner.

Scraps. Whatever falls off the dinner plate.

By this it should become apparent that the truth is Canada contains the North Pole. That's right Santaland.

Hockey is my favorite foreign sport. Well not anymore, however in Canada some of the kids are given the choice of studying to be goalkeeper or journalism (blubber salesmen).

Assume the kitty sleeping position. Then try to discover if there is something neck improving about that.

When you introduced me at your party as a director, you made it very easy for me to become popular. I had to say, "Everyone can be in a movie!"

I know what those people are all about. They have remarkable mouths for bad yen. I cannot believe the Master of Demons has not got wings.

Some greedy westerners recently downed the stock market just to obtain a better bond market. Thus funds to build new electric plants.

A raised eyebrow by the speaker during monologue means some vere is going to heck. A frown means vere in actors sick mind.

Rubbing the nose during opening monologue means, "How did he get those lines on?"

Be quiet! Self! Let the rich people go to rich people land.

Oh you know that on every set they serve food. It is everywhere.
[Sing] You're a kitty. You're a kitty.
And you wanna go outside.
When the birdies see ya comin
They all fly away to hide.

Come on kitty. Your sitting right on the ninth hole!

What? What is my reflection doing in the mirror?

I look kinda daffy in a suite, ain't I?

They invaded my shorty people room!

Is my dream house a mansion? No. Peabodio doesn't know why any of you want that considering the coming distaster.

Meows sound like: love me! Now! Translating apparently wasn't enough because now it wants to bite me. Until I sit up, legs crossed and ask, "Is this the one?" The next meow and smile sounds like yeah and it sits on my lap.

I know how to make it renovation. Cut a hole up to here. Put in a ladder and sell it for five times more than that sucker paid.

I knew these would be funny. The way they've hated my family for years. We put this barrier in front of our house so we could take cover while on guard duty.

Newsbreak: today the total number of suicides due to the recent stock market crash was recorded at town hall. For those seeking units, the list will be posted.

Transplant from my face to my bald head? She likes the idea. The only place they can get hair is from my ass. They could get it from my armpit too. I don't care. Who'll look for it?

I don't appear to Mulia as a vampire. Yet she fret, nat and sleeze. Hollywood's in a lot of pain after that take. Dodging all the snipers.

Peabodio

Nag Nag Nag Nag Nag!

Furniture that fits please. Short legs hanging over the side. Wide making the sofa like a love seat.

Newsflash: today the white spotlight debris of the rich and famous black athletes.

The car missed one of the Chicago's. That's good news. Don't ski drunk. Accidents like this occur in two's and three's.

I am not the guy they say I am. I am from New York. I am not one of those tattoos. No I don't! Think you guys should be buying body paint for your old mom?

Skank! Could it get any softer?

So stack some mobiles on top of each other at different angles so people can live in new after the athletes move out.

Portofino fantastic! It's not like Monte Carlo though. Monte Carlo's wealthy famous people. Portofino's wealthy without the fame Roy said.

I once heard a man tell a young woman that she'd form a band called Destiny's Child and become extremely successful. She told him she never really thought she'd do anything.

What a bunch of morons some people in the news media are. I love a kitty not a mess.

She sits in her house all day long waiting for blue pictures and poking herself with Mr. Dill. I ordered her to pull down her panties and prove that she was wet for men.

Actress play. Please not now!

They laughed at how many bags it does take to clear those others off the face of the planet.

She's suffering from extreme buttock dilemma. If you see her, do not attempt to apprehend her yourself.

Typical comment of an untreated mental case: "It seemed like a good idea at the time."

His immediate thoughts while watching the show Boot Camp, "Sassy actresses."

She wants to bee them all cold.

Then your family turns against you. Gets you fired. Puts you away and you still get angry if somebody blames them. How can you say anything else about one of them? Then he admits they've been coming on to him since he was ten and he's never had to work very hard at getting one of them.

I used to have a cell phone. I could sound the ringer. Instead of talking to myself, I made it sound and look like I was getting alot of calls. Latter I gave up the bit with the phone because I realized that all my relatives were walking around out there without cell phones.

Growdy nut wad! In other words that stinks!

Breaking news: The more you listen to the news, the fewer facts you hear.

Teenagers are enough of a problem without them clogging your drainage system.

In Hollywood, they have saying. Looking for a loud hit.

Your pet has been biting. It's exact thoughts are, "Who me? Your crazy!" Then your guest says, "Can you remove that cat?"
Is thinking that men were a constant problem with you? Did this develop in high school or since you've lived in town?

Hate: You puke! You smell! You blow hit!

I sure don't want to run into the drag in the locker room.

Some folks in the west are sitting there thinking, "Thank God they came from there!" Does that get them in? If your not sure how their related just use Ned's Pocket Dictionary to Genealogy.

Peabodio, Peabodio. Fisal, my son and daughter-in-law got their pictures on before I did. My dad used the a.k.a. Phil and use to say things like, "You are knott" on the radio.

Out in Missouri they're thinking, you know the water wasn't really that high.

I live in a trailer. Isn't that funny you bunch of rich behinds!

I've been to North Carolina. I've seen the sheep with racing numbers painted on their sides. Wonderful place yes.

You'll catch cold if you go topless is a Chech joke.

Being dianosed with prostrate cancer is the closest thing you'll ever get to playing baseball.

Soy friends be nice to me.

WB Weather, it's sure cold in New Hampshire.

Mary Poppins. Why isn't that a vere name?

Peabodio

Kiss my gritty and tell her to kiss mine too.

Every author does this. They stay up working on their book until they can't stay awake anymore. That's how the publisher knows they're an author.

CHAPTER FOUR

QUESTIONS

So what do you say to Nick after thirty minutes? Acting lessons paid off Nick.

Hobo asks why the house next to Ben's house isn't up for thoughts of foreclosure? Then he rounds the corner after taking in the residential block.

Let me go crazy because I forgot. Do you mind? The B.A. makes liars judgements and the Ph.D. knows better.

Explain this Swank, would you? It's just one of those wild things that comes out and rests peacefully on your shoulder.

Could you make electronic maid with less telephone wire please? The electronic dump some rich guy dumped on me yesterday was just too much.

Apply for a position with your own company, o.k.? The named former employer is the post office or the police but the reason for leaving has not been recorded. What did they do? By her, brought the telephone company down.

Do you know how to do when you laugh? Fold it in half and put it in your business.

How many days can you wear underwear without changing them asked Alamar? Three or six. Depends on whether or not you have a cold when you smell them.

How many rats does it take to fill a hole? It's a joke. The then the producer says that he's gonna kick some ass!

So what is Cordell? The sparter of the south?

Hey I ad-hey the sign, "Welcome to Georgia." Why not marry young and avoid the apes?

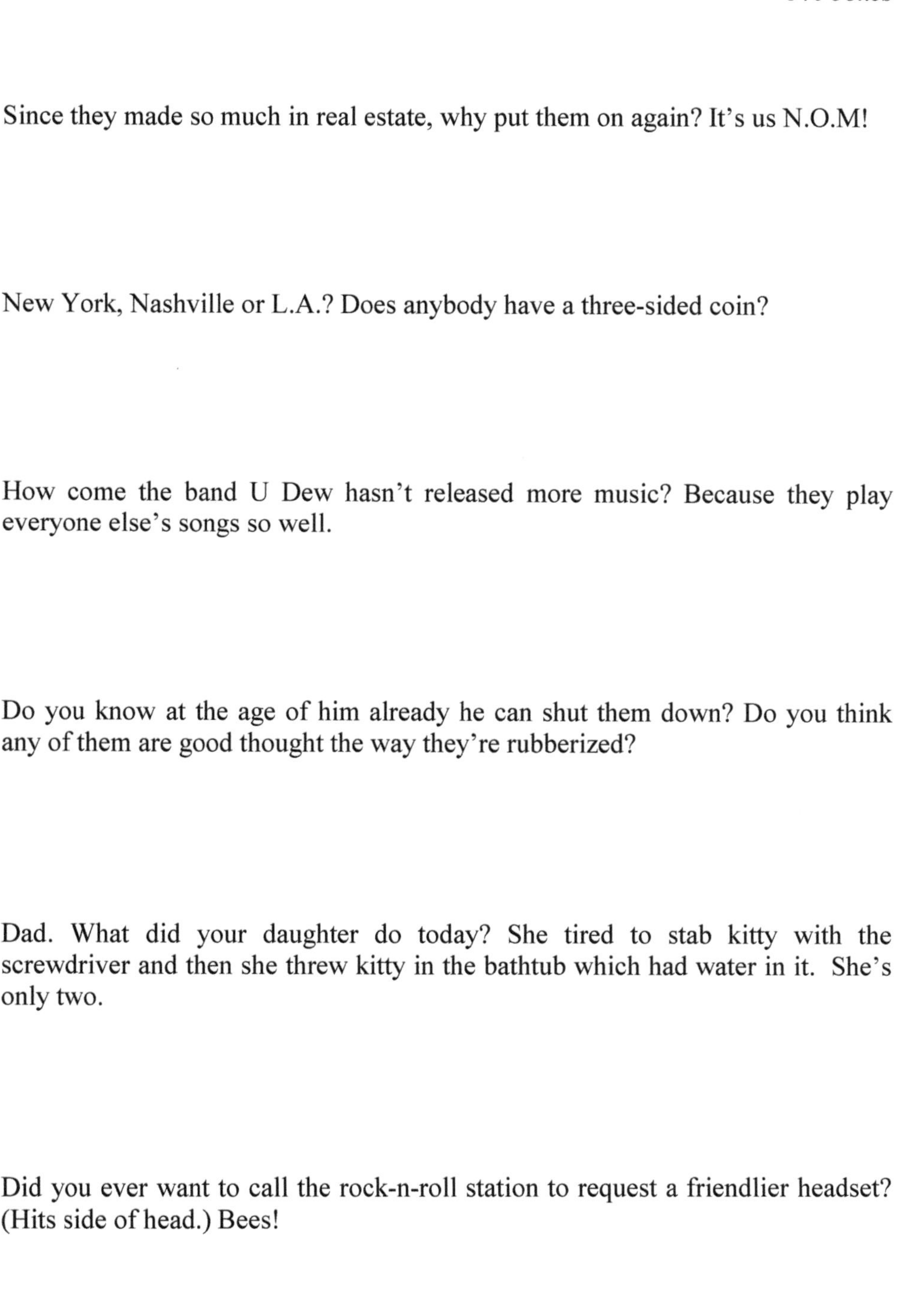

Since they made so much in real estate, why put them on again? It's us N.O.M!

New York, Nashville or L.A.? Does anybody have a three-sided coin?

How come the band U Dew hasn't released more music? Because they play everyone else's songs so well.

Do you know at the age of him already he can shut them down? Do you think any of them are good thought the way they're rubberized?

Dad. What did your daughter do today? She tired to stab kitty with the screwdriver and then she threw kitty in the bathtub which had water in it. She's only two.

Did you ever want to call the rock-n-roll station to request a friendlier headset? (Hits side of head.) Bees!

Who in L.A. said. “I don’t ever wake up for under one hundred-thousand dollars?”

You know that television show with the skeleton that pops up out of the coffin with that evil look? Well one day it opens and the animal rights pet skeleton pops up instead.

Please don’t act as if it was the ferrit who ripped off the ad agency’s idea. Did you hear them tape that?

Your neighbors doverman trainer noticed the crucifixes on your lawn. How could anyone miss those? They are all over the lawn. The customer answered, “I don’t see those.” So you adhere this. What do you say to the trainer? You know you’ve trained the dog.

What do some of you call your red hair? Why lie? It is not close to cherry, pumpkin or apple. It is orange. That is what it is closest to. Yet you say it will be the toast to the political. Your one of them. Why not just tear out your hair if you don’t like?

Did you ever see the episode where John-Boy takes the lumber in the face?

Do you enjoy being a robber? Well it pays the rent.

Why wasn't I arrested in Russia during the second revolution you ask? The soldiers took bribes.

What do you get when you cross Fedx with UPS? Fed Up.

Smell that? It's the order of a jail sentence.

How many of you have been fired for wearing the same clothing article as your boss? It's a common problem.

Why shouldn't I write a book about humor? They've laughed at me my whole life already.

Peabodio

How about a neon cactus for your wall. This is no longer unusual in Texas.

Did you ever mention a local contractor and obtain the interest of the young people? I've often thought that the only use the neighborhood mothers had for this man was to obtain jobs for hucks.

Your hispanic and you want to say your related to someone but you are not really? Your no dear.

Prison joke: a quick show of your hands please. Exactly how many of the guys are innocent?

Pasture in Bel Air. What happen to that?

Giving me bad vibes swaying skyscrapers?

Times gone on strike you say? What for? Shorter hours?

How many writers does it take to screw in a lightbulb? One to screw and fifty to forward all the calls around.

I didn't know he was an upperclassman from Berkeley. Did you see how that was run with it? That's the only way the stinking rich ever were.

Seattle musicians act strange around telephones. When it rings they'll say, "Why did it do that?"

I lost at musical chairs when I was small. They told me I was free to move around the country. What did he do? Go to school with an ad agency?

Did you see the one where Shat took the lumber in the head?

Peabodio

Why are there still undiagnosed actress exhibitionists? Let's go on this. I work at a bental hospital.

Why are some of us too mortified to rewind a Kilmer movie?

Listen insame in the membrain. Quite insane. Got no brain?

You think I am that way? I can tell you things about cows you never thought you needed to know before.

Then the underground army breaks into the radio station one day. Do you know how to use this thing because I have no idea whatsoever. [Sings.] Yeah ... I hope ya...

Some of you are sitting with your kitty wondering where the other paw pad was.

Copying the things you heard me say? Your right with that. You were taught to think for yourself weren't you?

How does Italian casting type cast? Italian or non-Italian?

How can you make it up to me? What has a picture of Grant on it and has been noted as a bribe?

You know how the Marines guard monuments standing perfectly still? So don't make fun of them when your in Washington because they are the stiffest.

Have you ever watched a show when the host has an outburst? The first thought I have always had is was the brandy bar still unlocked?

Have you ever been behind a panda when it let one go? In Washington, they describe this as panda art.

Peabodio

How can you tell which end smells bad on your pet? The food and the other smells the same.

Answers:
1. I've got pies for some of them.
2. Your going to die!
3. Your going to Hell or Alwife!
4. Haircut town.
5. They drove her to her death because she liked him.
6. Even tho you drummed up in a negative way, your comments created interest in my show so I'd like to actually thank the company.
7. There are a few: An evil actress pine pined by a corporate programmer; a sportscaster accused by the ivy league; an advertising mole who exits a talk show host or hostess; a manager who ousts the chief, whose ex-wife kisses the former half-off. Sound like anybody you know?
8. So many of the rich and famous steal, they all don't know that I meant somebody else when I did accuse.

The way they constantly do? Oh no ladies, I didn't sleep with anybody to get what I got. Unlike what I surmise is over fifty percent of you.

Transplant from my face to my bald head? She likes the idea. The place they can also get hair from is my ass. They could get it from my armpit too. I don't care. Who'll look for it?

What makes most of the actors run? Scriptwriters!

There is such a thing as being hugged to death. Ladies, why isn't that considered murder?

Would you say Boston under construction is something like Dresden in '45?

Have you ever felt like this? If the real estate agents aren't sellus of the house I'll be murderous of you?

Don't you want to call around a bit to get ideas before you go on the air?

Kizz face. Who knows who you were?

Who needs to be young when you breed ripe horse?

Peabodio

What's the matter Wee Wee? You can't keep your hands off yourself?

You oads do have your own milk, don't you?

CHAPTER FIVE

NIGHTCLUB

Intestinal fortitude means you've got guts not that you have big balls people. That is unless you live in Crystal City.

Beautiful people ask guess who wants them? Well I know they are more apt to become pornos unlike the rest of us.

So you debated your career with the public. I am not going to call them your fans tho. You said they wanted to see you in female undergarments.

Why do women want to put certain men in female cothing? I don't get it. What are these writers trying to say?

You made multi-millions of dollars a year. Why put on a dress?

When I sleep around, I don't know about it.

You know about the Rock-and-rock Hall of Fame? Make sure it's all dark.

If she gives up, she's wasting a hell of a pair.

I didn't know that Dave was the voice of the Mom Four.

Heart failure while making love. One second your saying oh God. The next second your saying hello Jesus.

Like a sheep.

So the way things are going, does kissing someones kiss mean deading it?

Love got fat then.

I am sure you know how I don't know because it's going on in your heads too.

Oh Nina! For crying out loud. Eek yourself off!

This is how I express anger. Want me to express lust?

Oh onion dog. Get out of my head! Don't write.

It reminds me of my old girlfriend Gena. She was so monthly, they sometimes shot at her. And on any given saturday night, they shot at her balcony.

I am just a poor boy without desert head.

You know the word that gives you instant social life? O.k. Susan, How could you forget me after last night?

A long time ago a famous female wanted to invent something that made men work for her. She invented what became known as the fireplace, to remind her of her father in hell. It's not romantic to work while you are trying to have sex ladies. You can hear her. "Could you get some more wood from the forest before you wipe that thing out dear?"

Hear me. That displays this is the cry those Hispanics are and it's related to him constantly by women. He says to her. "Come lay with me in my country villa today and we'll say you did lie with me two months ago in Chicago."

What's a matter for you dud noodle breath?

Short on the motzzarella for a fella.

Eyes closed. Do you see her? The girl of your dreams. What has happened to her lately? She has black breast problem. An erection is sticking out from her neck and the lips hangs almost to the floor.

I never made it with a hole? Think maybe they got carried a away do ya?

I am so sick of group minded women. Do they ever finish a sentence by themselves? It is their fault that I don't care which one of then I insult. Could it be that is too much stick on their minds? Right over the barrel on that one.

Hambone. It's not my fault. It's her Mars tormented little ovaries.

You've heard them say, "That's the way they do it?" Then say, "And you don't mean anything pre-marital by that!" That's just about covering it.

Hotter then pepper spray. I'll pull my pants down lady so don't spray me the body, without it all down there, was found at Hispanic Pond.

The rest of it I wouldn't leave on your message machine.

If you don't skip rasping on my wife you won't know. If you do you could be dead. The man who didn't think this was funny obviously doesn't listen to women talk all day long.

The industrial job that I discovered was the most secretive was #1. C.I.A. #2. Porno. I figured the latter infiltrated the former. The first time I told this joke I got these telephone calls. How come they also had the telephone numbers of the female porno stars? I asked for those. Sell them to ya for ten bucks.

She peace piped me and you don't acknowledge raid hers.

Rotten mouth. She smiled with all her teeth though.

The big chill auds out. The chill factor auds out.

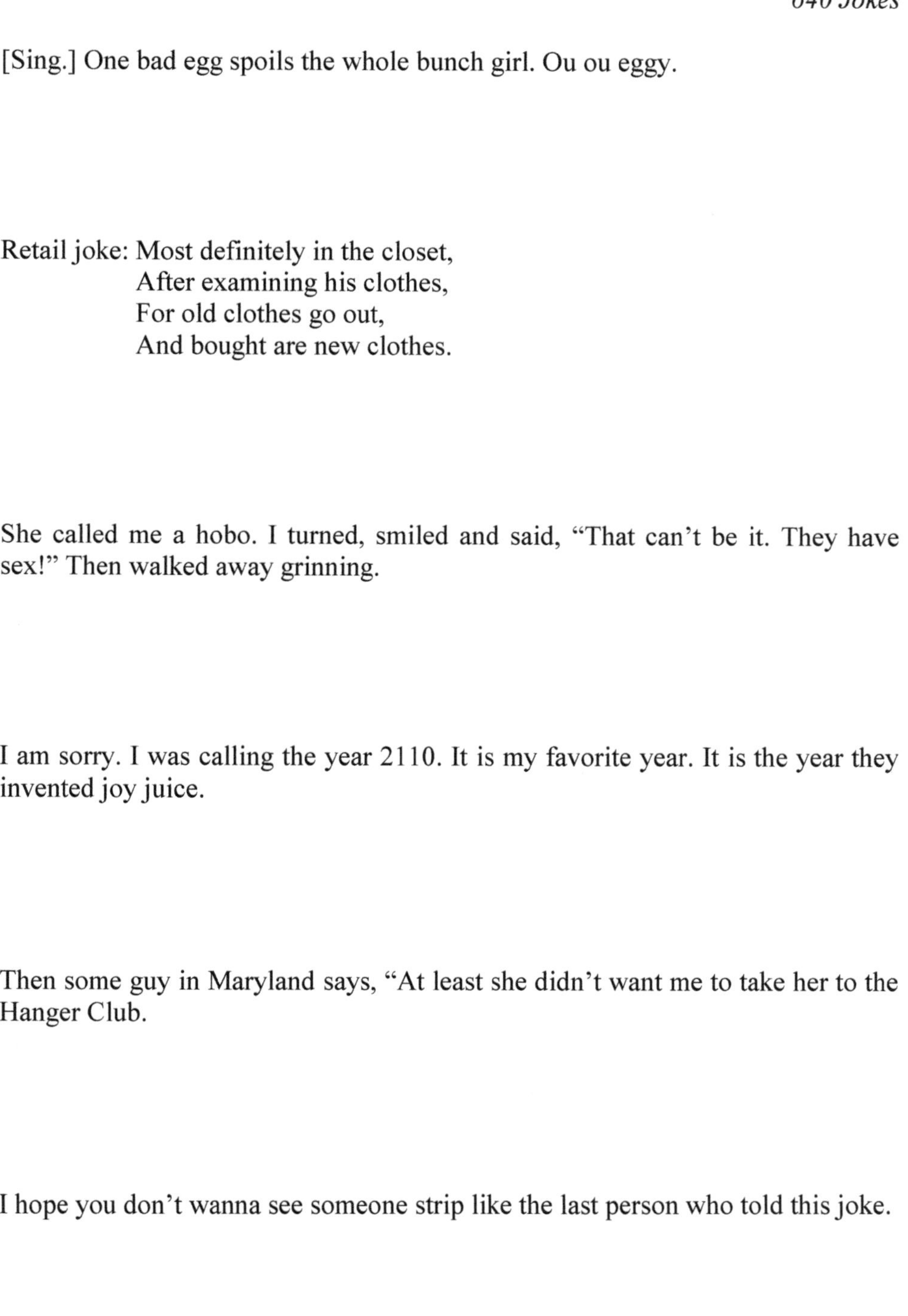

[Sing.] One bad egg spoils the whole bunch girl. Ou ou eggy.

Retail joke: Most definitely in the closet,
After examining his clothes,
For old clothes go out,
And bought are new clothes.

She called me a hobo. I turned, smiled and said, "That can't be it. They have sex!" Then walked away grinning.

I am sorry. I was calling the year 2110. It is my favorite year. It is the year they invented joy juice.

Then some guy in Maryland says, "At least she didn't want me to take her to the Hanger Club.

I hope you don't wanna see someone strip like the last person who told this joke.

Black bush, white bush, black bush, white bush, pretty little bush bush. Somehow you also know Urkel, didn't come up with this.

Oh it's that hopeless creature at the end of the street. Looking for a buck?

See you on your roller skates you hasty girl. She doesn't care about ham. He only cares about hers.

You have aggressive sexual anger. Something he can fun lip to her.

What drip makes Lee Krasner clap?

The housemother of four females was proud that it took six months before the propane tank ran out. Some guy out there will brag that he caused half of that.

Does he have anything to hang onto? Yes. He pulled it out for her.

Thank-you. You're frame from cot sizing on us.

Chuck said, "When he's polish, that amounts to a poll job."

You women haven't thought this thing through enough. To be a bitch is really a good thing. They are precieved as loyal. They want to be with those that feed them. They are friendly. They want to be pet. They don't romp and rough house like the male. So you see it's a compliment and you all take the word the wrong way.

Since she doesn't have sense enough to hose. Why hose her?

Way-o sorry, I am not Dayo fart!

Cucumber joke writer wrote that his was bigger then that and I also wrote the scene about how I got it in by saying I don't write for fruit.

Peabodio

Why doesn't she desire him? She stands in judgment of his dick. Programs him. After the verdict, and after the tingles are gone, she dies.

Noodle breath. You have noodles for brains.

Egg roll head! You have egg roll for head!

Your not really coming into your own. Your from Yonkers.

You can't tell me I fart for L.A.!

Too bad you marved. I'd clean you off with my tongue.

Producer joke: you know how it is. Your posing in the window one day. Thought you'd get in some ogleing, when ...

Three, four, fish fish. Orange yellow green fish.

Your not turning me into a frig-it angel punk!

Skinny!

Rat protection!

Run away from the vere and famous producers.

So you didn't think that was funny. I just wanna bee. I just wanna be on really, really, really bad o.k.? Got a prob do ya?

I wasn't sure what to call this section. Heading ideas were "sex", "running free", or "bad jokes".

The sun must be bad today because I saw a women sweating like a postitute in church. Mousetrap.

I woke up this morning realized my girlfriend wasn't there. Things really looked dark and the whole world seemed stinking rotten. Then the dog rolled off my face. Yes sir rubber dog. Aggar(d).

Snake. Bag of bones stupefied.

Some of the hos have been demanding advertisements for vagina cream and here it is. Try draino.

Good kid. Come out alright. It's about time people made friends with your face and not your mulitt. Come out, toys of the closet!

I don't regret kicking you out of the closet. Your girlfriend tells you things you shouldn't feel real bad about that. No one in the closet was as horny as you were.

I am going to get some fake breasts, some polyester slacks and wig hair and I am going to throw a tupperware party all by myself.

Considering thankful was really one of the cleverest lines. Do lesbians really want to hug her? Or is it one of those run their hand down her side things?

Who's heard that New York City banned Fool and Nofind groups from marching in the St. Patrick's Day show last year? Boston just couldn't stand that New York was far more conservative so this year they also banned them.

By come out of the closet, they mean, not from behind the closet but from behind the struggle.

If you were called anything that reminds them of the word queer, it is likely that you had already applied for a job at Viacom and you had been rejected.

New Orleans women always notice the big ones.

Hug your mutter. Hug your vatter. Just don't say which one is hotter.

Sometimes, when I think they're going to do it right on television, I can't look.

When interviewing the pornos, they find out that at some point they've all done it either way during the intercourse of their careers. No wonder New York!

I don't know what to tell people in Los Angeles. The rest of the world sent you the fools. Many of you don't know that the rest of the world isn't like that or surrounded by that environment.

La Freak shook his ass on Regis. He knows not to do that again. Day after Superbowl. We've seen about enough!

Jamoo lepra got freaky all night long!

Exactly how much flour did you have to use to fluff her?

You've seen this ad. All white meat! Give it to me baby! Ninety-nine cent!

Shirt. I am the guy who got Cherry to chirp.

Even the freakiest gals in this city get a lot of guys.

My wife ask me if a female who sleeps around is a slut, what is the equivalent name for a man who does the same thing? None of them really sleeps around or even though some do sleep around, they are not sluts or just call him the same thing no lie.

Who'll ever forget unpredictable Marty, whose done everything including the kitchen sink naked.

Ashcroft doesn't screw anyone but his wife.

The fromp came to the guy at the bar asking him, "Wanta hump a pretty actress?" He answered the fromp right away, "Sure, where is she?"

I know to feel her down there. Horney Goat Weed.

Mighty moo-lady shows us twinkie!

It's about time someone made friends with your face and not your ass.

When there's bad news on the home front think pharmaceutic stock.

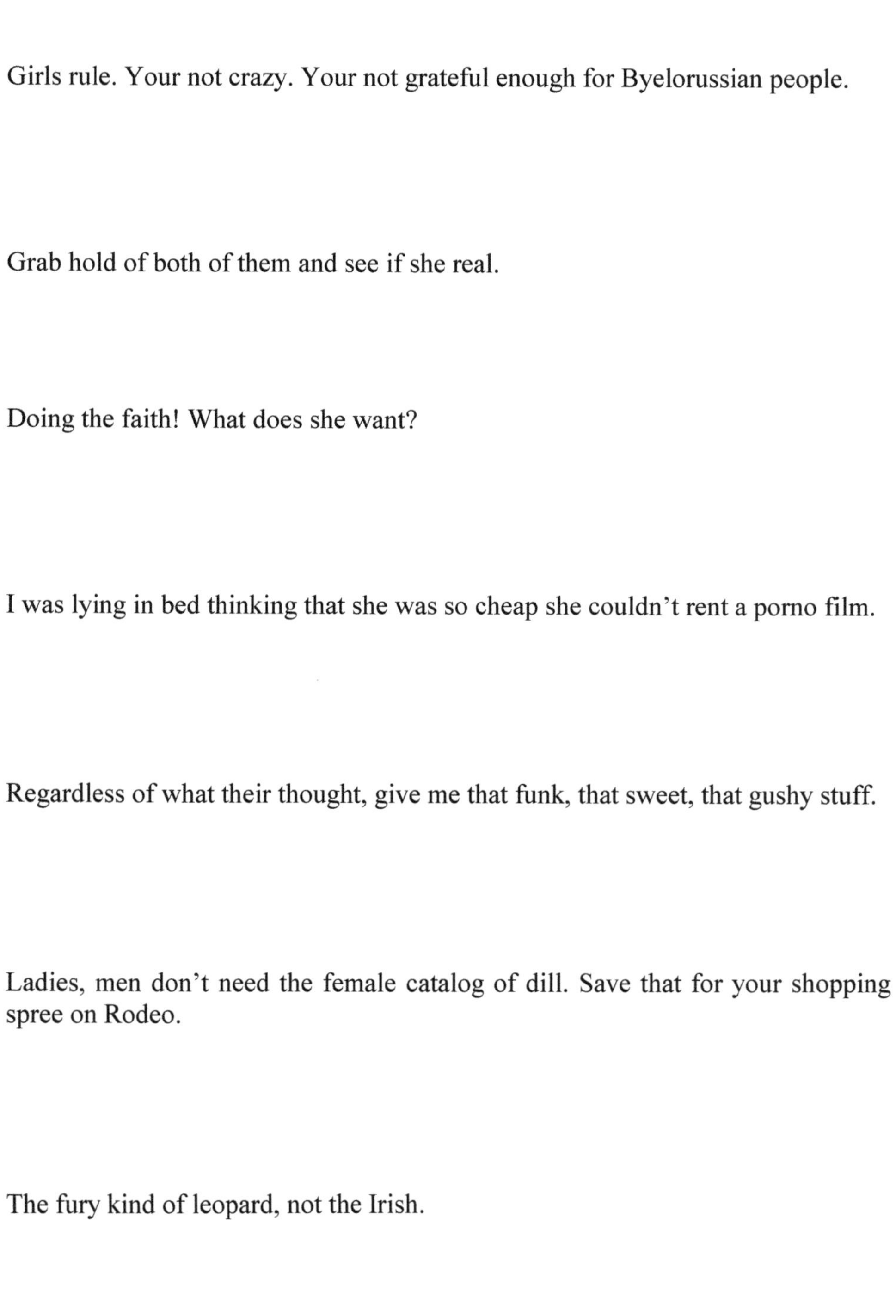

Girls rule. Your not crazy. Your not grateful enough for Byelorussian people.

Grab hold of both of them and see if she real.

Doing the faith! What does she want?

I was lying in bed thinking that she was so cheap she couldn't rent a porno film.

Regardless of what their thought, give me that funk, that sweet, that gushy stuff.

Ladies, men don't need the female catalog of dill. Save that for your shopping spree on Rodeo.

The fury kind of leopard, not the Irish.

It was one of those "BC" networks. The announcer just had to put the act down as if he was a programming executive making a billion dollars a year. When they barged in, they found him on top of Miss _____.

Well then come here. I am so very pleased we are going to have all the sex. You look very bendy wise hole.

Do you know what it's like? Standing next to you in the elevator? Keep your hands where I can see them at all times!

If you hear the word "queer" your either watching SNL or MTV. So why were you spying?

Almonds are in every crunch bear fruit.

When there's bad news on the home front think pharmaceutic stock.
She really is a pug faced bull dyck!

When it comes to the contractor set, you know how there's famous.

Hobo's at home thinking that, "selling egg" really means selling sex.

I'd beg for her. So she says roll over and play dead.

CHAPTER SIX

STORIES

Many years ago I went to a museum party with some colleages of mine. We drank wine and ate cheese. It was one of those houses that was open to the public but because of connections we held our party there that afternoon. Then someone sat down in a chair and broke it. When we found out that the chair was worth $25,000., all anybody could do was laugh.

When competing we try anything to win. Even using that kid that always sits alone in the playground. Latter, we start telling people that we are more successful then we really are. And last, we stuff our clothing. There we are. So I am the one who was alone, who stuffed and told everyone I won the lottery. So what?

I went sailing in the Atlantic Ocean one weekend with a buddy from work. On the way into the slip we got pulled over by the Coast Guard for a dingy equipment violation. When we got to the dock, the female reporter was waiting on the pier. When I ask her to keep the report out of the newspaper I found out we were both dating her at the same time.

It seems some guy heard the play and went out and poured tar all over the excavation. Put up a sign and now charges tourists five dollars to see them. It is not true that the man had a daughter named La Braya Tarr. Nore is it true that this is her grave site.

I was listening to Free Falling by what's his name the singer, in the living room one evening before dinner. Laughing at the guitar adhere, my girlfriend comes into the room says, "He knows something. He knows something. See I told you," so the people in the other room could hear. To this day I don't know what she was talking about but I am convinced it has to do with lyrics from this song. Every time it comes on I turn to look at her face for a reaction. She smiles.

When I was growing up, we lived in a house in the american average suburbs like a lot of folks. It was just that my mother came from a small town miles away where the larger houses held the same price tag. One day after the yearly visit, I ask why not just move there and be the best of? Mom said that she often felt that way too and turned to Dad, who put his hand on his chin in dadly fashion and answered, "And all your relations move in all around. How many do you think they'd be?" [Requested use of they'd be.] Mom answered him three times over the years. The first answer was none. A couple of years latter the answer was twenty-two. The year after that somebody came up with three hundred twenty-two.

I went to one of those countries where there were sheep grazing along the roadway. One field had a billboard advertising the race track. Some of the sheep had numbers painted on them.

I once had a math teacher who asked on the call-a-round how he could maintain the attention of his classes. Knowing he was seriously expecting an answer I suggested that his comedy also be quite serious. Since he was known to sit on his desk facing the class waste paper basket prearranged thus. So one day my after talking at length about Edipus, he jumped off the desk from where he was sitting. Placing one foot hence also one leg, into the metal wastebasket. Looking down, shaking it off, he did not miss more then one sylibus of his lecture and continued to notify the class of the homework assignment amid roaring laughter. Hence, the only teacher I know of to admit that he was a basket case.

You should have no reason to claim the system in this county has failed. On the contrary, the mandate to test the system has proved it worthy. This would not have happened in the new Europe, since the democracy wars, without mild protest and some shooting. The major disruption regarding the Bush/Gore Florida election results occurred in the newsroom, where there was some pushing and bad words. Can you see your favorite news anchors shooting at each other? While the conflict in Florida was never anticipated by colonial minds, the newsroom situation was. Remember, the close result legal issue had already been tested years ago in the Provo cheeze-belt with very little hype.

CHAPTER SEVEN

I. O. POEMS

ADt

There once was a man named Hochrod
Who lived in the time of Ad
Or was that in the town of Od?
Anyway we know that he was a grape farmer
In the hills above the Fine River
That were left by his maternal grandmother Cher
Who vacationed at Cernaut.

When Hoch reached the age of 51
He went to visit friends in March Morava
And never went back to Od.
All his family and son Radet thought
Was that he was imprisioned or killed.
He wasn't
He died of natural causes
After he witnessed
Heindall of the bridge slay Loki
On that fact you can count, no joki.

Limerick

There was once a maiden of Siam
  Who said to her lover, young Kiam,
    If you kiss me, of course,
    You will have to use force,
But God knows you are stronger than I am.

Orange Breast (are you color blind?)

Robin flys up to the branch from the forest ground
  A little less fat after laying the eggs she found,
    Cleans worm juice off on the branch,
    This creature takes no chance,
Then flys into the sky without a sound.

Hankering

My life, my way, no stopping me.
How did she get into it?
She couldn't get enough.
Hiss at the hansome guy,
All the girls are crazy for,
That's the life.

Figures

– so what would make the difference?
true at all ... Why should any account differ
In the end; juggle the figures a little
Filter decimals, engross the statement,
Gives you much more confidence
To live on the morrow
The flight leaves at 10:07 a.m.
Packed, two.

Flower of the Nile

Halibut of the Indian Ocean,
Desert overland Africa by jeep, by camel,
Flower of the Nile, river of many waters,
Sea lily of the Mediterranean,
Kasadasi of ancient places,
You Rachel pilgrim to the Holy Land,
you Rachel.

Spin

Spin around and click your heels,
That's the way Dorothy feels.
Dorothy, Dorothy, Dorothy, Dorothy.
Spin around and click your heels,
That's the way Dorothy feels.

Zoo

Well if they're going to stare
Like I am a zoo caged animal
On display for the crowd there
Fed in front of runny nose kindred
Pacing back and forth, to and fro
The bars dividing the viewing space so
Impeding the scenery, then rust.
If they're going to leave me to die
In this prison gone public; my own zoo
Show that never goes on the road
Concrete oasis hot house too: shoot!

Imagine (the original)

Imagine erasing any skepticism
Of slogan, pageantry or integrity
Unwinding constant cynicism
Spoonfed idea exhaustion
Dispel sincere dialogue from media forces
Doubtful in-depth-journalism
Susceptible to alien invasion.
Perfect blend of sacrifice and hopefulness.
Incisive dormant post modern meditation or
Cognac supreme disgust establishment.

Hump

This cherished and passionate laughter of theirs,
Shows me the crisp tranquil autumn.
Then becons him toward those swan ponded lanes,
Meadows of wild roses, lilac and lilies.
Sunny lawn among them, she finds the perfect spot.
Prelude to her silky satin entrance alter.
She displays enchantment gratefully lover.
Visit the country harvest described as art.
Then the defined man, scrubbable, forever durable.
Not headed for the claw toothed shredder.
Set adrift, yet they are only ripples upon the surface.
Expected gentlemen, hero, her guardian always.
She urges the entanglement, then commands it.
Embracing tumblers, roll, toss, tussel about.
Bold strength, determined domination sequesters
Laughing nuisance nuzzling reconciling herself.
Tugs were really her instinctive gravity,
Awaken, brought to the surface, lover's surge.

Fruit of the lake

Boat across water, blue, dark and deep,
The journey, a memory, ours to keep.
Fish below us, only clouds up above,
This ain't the trip on Hawk or Dove.
We stop to have lunch that you brought,
It's not a basket but bag of art,
Thoughtful dear hag, al-la-cart.
Darn good cooking for the old fart.
You ask me then about when we were young,
Wondering if you were the only chum.
I laugh at you, knowing you'll cry,
You'll never know, snake in your eye.

Blues Baby

Keep the body not the man
Keep the body not the man
You know mama cut you loose
So run as fast as you can.

Lose your job to a better man
Lost your job to a better man
Your boss done cut you down
Run on home fast as you can.

Taken away by the man
Taken away by the man
Easier to catch you at home
Nobody cares if your the right man.

Peabodio

Pooky Poo

I am playing banjo at grama's house.
I am playing banjo at grama's house
I am playing banjo at grama's house
On the lake, on the lake.

Magic fountain was her way
Magic fountain was her way
Magic fountain was her way
I am magic fountain all my life.

Pook-ee pook-ee pok
Pook-ee pook-ee pok
Pook-ee pook-ee pok
Pook pook pooky poo.

Don't feel her up, put her down
Don't feel her up, put her down
Don't feel her up, put her down
Magic fountain goes to heck.

Ding Dong Song

Christmas, Christmas, sky is black
Stars shine so bright up so high.
Sleep, I'm the elf they call Sleepy
I live way up there in Santa Land
We've all been working oh so hard.
To make this one day holiday grand.

Every year snow blankets the town.
The town that black Christmas knows.
Lights reflect still and bright glows.
Tis Christmas time jolly he knows.
The snow has fallen about knee deep.
Come sip cider by the fireplace keep.

Da da da, da da da da da.
Da da, da da da da da.
Ding dong ding ding ding dong.

I'll be on Santa's sleigh this year.
When it leaves from the north pole dear.
The road filled with deep snow ahead.
Sled on over to the old homestead.
We'll wave to all those we pass by Jack.
On bell-collared horse named Hack.
[1]

[1] One Way Music/GDPC

About the Author

When SNL Studios credited him for the lyrics of a hit song, he knew it was time to market this book. Published here are many jokes he wrote, which were used by comedians on nearly every comedy show of the past decade. Some appeared on radio, television, or in movies. Sometimes the only credit he got was on-the-air credit, as with SNL.

Some of the jokes published in this book have remained very popular. So much so they were recycled by the humor industry.

Peabodio has no fear. He has blazed his own path. The reception of his work has been pretty good; three of his first five jokes were used on television. Although his work is dissimilar and moody, he doesn't have a problem talking about it. "I basically woke up one day in 1995 and started typing. So I am not the fastest network material, or am I? Just ask programming." Then he smiles and wonders how long it will take for someone to leave a message. He is happy to write jokes that people can relate to, whoever they are. "I'll always write jokes." He says they are part of him.

His status? Single, married, a parent, grandfather, divorced, widower and a New Yorker. Writing jokes started as a lark. A way to impress the producers and directors. You may also purchase ***Peabodio's Joke Tron Show*** on compact disk.

www.ingramcontent.com/pod-product-compliance
Ingram Content Group UK Ltd.
Pitfield, Milton Keynes, MK11 3LW, UK
UKHW041937190726
13854UKWH00004B/1649